THE MIGHTY HIPPOPOTAMUS

BY SUSAN EVENTO

MONDO

Special thanks to our consultant, Stephen K. Krueger, a biologist and zookeeper
in the Large Mammal Department at the Toledo Zoo in Toledo, Ohio.

Photo and Illustration Credits: Cover, p. 26: © Steve Bloom/stevebloom.com; p. 1: © David C. Fritts/Animals Animals; pp. 2, 3, 30, 31, and 32:
© corbisstockmarketcom; pp. 4-5: © Joe McDonald/Animals Animals; p. 6 (top): © A. & M. Shah/Animals Animals; p. 6 (center): © Tom
Brakefield/CORBIS; p. 6 (bottom): © Root, AOSF/Animals Animals; pp. 7 (top), 22: Anup Shah/Animals Animals; pp. 7 (bottom), 16:
© Zig Leszczynski/Animals Animals; p. 9 map: © 2003 by Charlie Hunt; p. 10: © Tim Fitzharris/Minden Pictures; p. 11: © Bradley Smith/Animals
Animals; p. 12: © Bruce Davidson/Animals Animals; p. 13: © Chris Johns/Getty Images, Inc.; p. 14: © Dani/Jeske/Animals Animals; p. 15:
© Martin Harvey; p. 17: © Ingrid Van Den Berg/Animals Animals; p. 18: © Mark Deeble & Victoria Stone/OSF; p. 19: © Mitsuaki Iwago/Minden
Pictures; p. 20: © E.R. Degginger/Color-Pic. Inc.; p. 21: © Mike Wilkes/naturepl.com; p. 23: © Frans Lanting/Minden Pictures; p. 24: © Klaus-Peter
Wolf/Animals Animals; p. 25: © Linda S. Milks; p. 27: © Anup Shah/naturepl.com; p. 28: © Phyllis Greenberg/Animals Animals; p. 29:
© Topham/The Image Works.

For information contact:
MONDO Publishing
980 Avenue of the Americas
New York, NY 10018
Visit our website at www.mondopub.com

Printed in China

10 11 12 13 14 PB 9 8 7 6 5 4 3 2
10 11 12 13 14 SP 9 8 7 6 5 4 3 2 1

ISBN 1-59034-493-6 (PB)   ISBN 1-60175-768-9 (SP)

Designed by Charlie Hunt

Library of Congress Cataloging-in-Publication Data

Evento, Susan.
The mighty hippopotamus / Susan Evento.
v. cm.
Contents: Introduction : hippo highlights – Family Hippopotamidae – Where in the world? – Physical characteristics – Foraging
and diet – Grooming – Social organization and behavior – Mating and reproduction – Hippo culture, past and present.
ISBN 1-59034-493-6 (pbk.)
1. Hippopotamidae–Juvenile literature. [1. Hippopotamus.] I. Title.

QL737.U57 E9 2003
599.63'5—dc21   2002190718

CONTENTS

Introduction: Hippo Highlights

Hippopotami are enormous mammals. And as you are about to find out they are enormously interesting, too. Surprisingly little is known about these larger-than-life creatures. We do know, however, that hippos are fast runners and fierce fighters, and that they move gracefully through the water.

In Greek the name hippopotamus means "river horse"—although hippos aren't related to horses at all. Because hippos have physical features that are similar to pigs' and like to wallow in mud, some scientists thought they were related to the pig family. Recently discovered fossils, however, show that hippos are most closely related to whales and dolphins, whose ancestors used to walk on land.

Hippos are most active at night. During the night they travel well-worn paths, eating grass for five to six hours. Then, before the sun and temperature rise, they retreat to their cool daytime water habitat. There they wallow or sleep standing up, sometimes resting their huge heads on one another as if they were pillows.

After a night spent eating large amounts of grass, hippos eliminate huge amounts of waste into the water. Their waste, called dung, sets up an ecosystem in the rivers and lakes where they spend their lazy days. Tiny organisms feed on the hippos' dung. Then larger animals feed on those tiny organisms.

5

Red-billed oxpeckers eat the ticks and leeches on a hippo's skin, helping to clean the large animal.

Hippos can run up to 30 miles (48 km) per hour on land and move gracefully underwater.

Besides supporting life in rivers and lakes, hippos provide food for small creatures like the oxpecker, a type of bird. Hippos also become temporary homes for leeches and other parasites. In addition to all the animals that live on and around hippos, many hippos themselves live in groups, sometimes called bloats.

In spite of their enormous size and weight, hippos move surprisingly well. Most scientists believe that hippos get around in the water by walking along the river- or lake-bottom. In deep water, hippos actually move forward by jumping—using their hind legs to push off the bottom. They are good divers, climbers, and runners. In fact, hippos have been clocked running as fast as 30 miles (48 km) per hour on land—nearly twice as fast as a human can run.

When their territory or young is threatened, hippos can become vicious. Many explorers and hunters have had boating accidents involving hippos. Hippos can bite a small boat in half with their large, gaping mouths and razor-sharp teeth. They aren't the gentle giants they may appear to be.

Family Hippopotamidae

Today, two different types of hippopotami exist—the common, or river, hippopotamus (*Hippopotamus amphibius*) and the pygmy hippopotamus (*Hexaprotodon liberiensis*). The two species make up the family Hippopotamidae.

The pygmy hippopotamus is much smaller than the common hippopotamus. It is also much rarer, so less is known about it. The pygmy species was discovered in the 1840s, but it wasn't until the 1980s that scientists were able to obtain information about how this animal lives in the wild. By day, pygmy hippos are well hidden by the dense cover of rainforests and swamps. And darkness makes their nighttime behavior difficult to observe. Pygmy hippos spend less of their lives in the water than do common hippos.

The word "hippopotamus" actually has two correct plurals: hippopotamuses and hippopotami.

Common hippopotamus (Hippopotamus amphibius)

Pygmy hippopotamus (Hexaprotodon liberiensis)

7

Where in the World?

Paleontologists have found hippo fossil deposits in Europe, Asia, and Africa from the late Miocene to late Pleistocene eras (10 million to 10,000 years ago). These fossil records indicate that there were once several species of hippos and that they lived in many more areas than today's hippos do.

About 2,000 years ago, the common hippo still lived in almost every river south of the Sahara Desert in Africa. However, over time, its numbers decreased rapidly. During the eighteenth century, the hippo became very rare in the Nile Delta. This was because farmers turned much of the hippos' territory into cropland. Then, when hippos ate or trampled their crops, the farmers shot them. In addition, native people and hunters killed hippos for their meat and tusks. The last hippos in Egypt were killed by about 1816.

Hippos continue to be killed for destroying crops and for their meat and tusks. Compared to other animals, a much larger portion of a hippo's body is edible, making it an excellent meat source. Hippos' tusks, especially the males' lower canines, can be as large as some elephant tusks. They look very much like elephant ivory, but they do not yellow with age as elephant tusks do.

Today, many hippos live in parks or reserves where they are protected. Common hippos are currently found in rivers and lakes in West and East Central Africa. This is a very small part of the area where they used to live. These days, certain areas seem overpopulated with common hippos, but that's only because the hippos that are left crowd together in smaller areas as their habitat shrinks.

Pygmy hippos are found in areas of Liberia, the Ivory Coast, Sierra Leone, and Guinea—all in Africa. They live in lowland forests and swamps, sometimes finding shelter in tunnels or hollows dug along the banks of streams. Pygmy hippos live in areas that are difficult to patrol. Loggers and farmers destroy the pygmy hippos' habitat, and hunters kill them for their meat. Their small habitat continues to shrink. Laws have been passed protecting pygmy hippos from extinction, but they continue to become less and less common in the wild.

Common hippos can live as long as 40 years in the wild and up to 50 years in captivity.

Beginning in the mid-1800s, hippos were brought to zoos around the world, and many still live in zoos today. In 1903 a hippo named Peter the Great was born at the Central Park Zoo in New York City. This popular hippo lived to be 49½ years old and, for many years, held the record for being the longest-living hippo in captivity. But in 1995, Tanga, a hippo at a zoo in Germany, died at the ripe old age of 61!

In 1927, President Calvin Coolidge received a pygmy hippo as a gift. He named the hippo Bill. Today, almost all the pygmy hippos living in American zoos are descendants of Bill.

= PYGMY HIPPO

= COMMON HIPPO

Physical Characteristics

After the elephant, the common hippo rivals the rhinoceros as the second heaviest land mammal on Earth. Some adult hippos weigh a whopping 7,000 pounds (3,175 kg)—about the same weight as a large pickup truck! Hippos have huge heads, short necks, and long, barrel-shaped bodies. They grow up to 15 feet (4.6 m) long, but with their short, stumpy legs, common hippos stand only around five feet (1.5 m) tall at the shoulders. Their short tails are around 15 inches (38 cm) long.

The common hippo's eyes, ears, and nose are high up on its large face. The position of these features allows it to see, hear, and breathe while all of its body and most of its head are underwater. When a hippo goes underwater, its nose and ears close. It can hold its breath and stay underwater for five or six minutes at a time. As the hippo resurfaces, its nostrils open to exhale and its ears spring back up. Hippos can sleep in the water because their bodies automatically rise to the surface when they need to breathe.

Hippos can smell, see, and hear quite well. Scientists think that hippos are able to communicate with one another both on land and in the water. They make a variety of sounds that are believed to be different types of messages.

The common hippo has webbed feet to help it move in the water and broad nails that help it grip the bottoms of rivers and lakes as it walks underwater. Each foot has four padded toes that support its massive body. Although the hippo has short legs, it can run faster than a person, make quick turns, and climb steep riverbanks. Hippos don't even bother stepping over obstacles in their way—they just barrel right through them!

◄ *The position of the common hippo's eyes, ears, and nose allows it to keep most of its body underwater while remaining aware of its surroundings.*

The common hippo's skin is smooth and thick. It is brownish-gray to bluish-black in color on the top and pinkish on the underside. The hippo's skin is well-suited for its environment in some ways, but not in others. Its outer layer of skin absorbs water easily when it's in the water, which is important in the hot, dry African climate. However, the hippo loses much of its moisture through its skin—more, in fact, than any other mammal. The hippo's skin is constantly absorbing and losing water.

Like most other mammals (but unlike humans), hippos don't sweat to regulate their body temperature. However, they do produce a sticky pinkish-red fluid, which is thought to moisturize and protect their skin from harmful sun rays. It was once thought that hippos actually sweated blood! The liquid is also thought to protect against infection because hippos' wounds don't get infected, even in the muddy water of wallows and lakes.

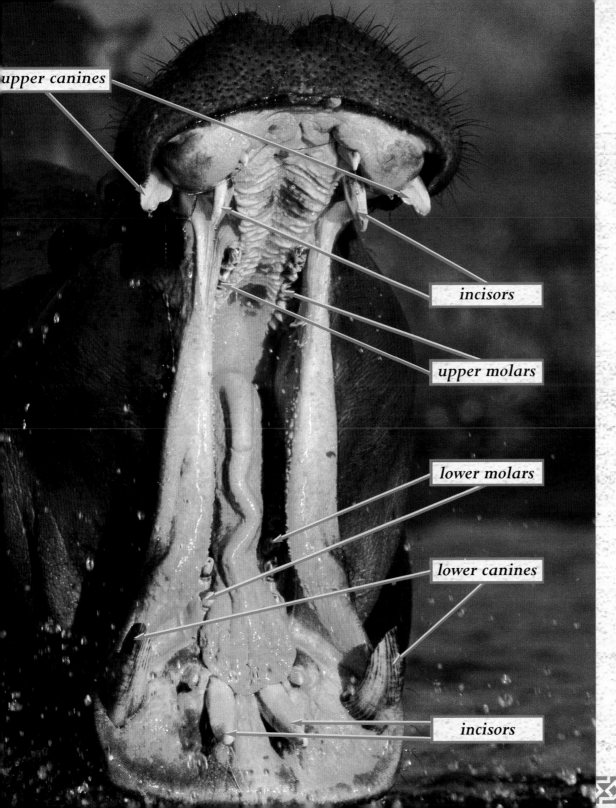

upper canines

incisors

upper molars

lower molars

lower canines

incisors

The common hippo's mouth is a wonder. It can open three to four feet (.9 to 1.2 m) wide, nearly 150°! A hippo has 34 to 36 teeth. Its tusk-like incisors and canine teeth grow throughout its life but are continually worn down through use. The lower canine teeth, the largest of its tusk-like teeth, point upward and can extend 20 inches (.5 m) beyond the gum line. The hippo's lips are about two feet wide.

In the 1700s, hippo tusks were used to make false teeth. George Washington, the first president of the United States of America, had teeth made of hippo tusks, not wood!

The pygmy hippo looks like a young common hippo in size and build, but its legs and neck are proportionately longer. Its skin is darker than the common hippo's—greenish-black on top, gray on the sides, and lighter on the underside. An adult pygmy hippo can weigh up to 605 pounds (275 kg) and reach a height of three feet (.9 m) at the shoulder. Together, its head and body can reach a length of six feet (1.8 m), and its tail is around six inches (15 cm) long.

The pygmy's head is smaller than the common hippo's, and its eyes are positioned more to the side of the head. Like the common hippo, the pygmy's body is hairless except for the bristles on its mouth, nose, lips, and tail (which is bushier than the common hippo's). Like its larger relative, the pygmy produces a sweat-like fluid that makes it slick to the touch. As with the common hippo, the liquid is thought to moisturize and protect its skin from harmful sun rays, as well as prevent infection.

The pygmy hippo has broad, sharp nails, and its teeth are every bit as sharp as those of the common hippo.

Only a pygmy hippo's front feet are webbed, and they are not as webbed as the common hippo's. Its tusk-like lower canine teeth serve as weapons and, along with its lips, help cut down plants. Pygmies are also very graceful both on land and in the water. They, too, have the ability to hold their breath underwater for minutes at a time while walking on the bottom of streams and swamps.

Foraging and Diet

At night, common hippos climb out of the water to graze for up to six hours. They follow paths, called grazing trails, which many of them enter and exit in the same place every night. These loops, marked by piles of their dung, are usually about two to seven miles (3.2 to 11.3 km) long. The exact purpose of the dung piles isn't known, but they are thought to help guide the hippo along its nightly grazing path.

In spite of the hippo's large mouth and sharp teeth, it mostly eats short land grasses, cropping them with its broad, rough lips. Sometimes hippos pull out so much grass along the edges of the river that the water erodes the riverbank, and gullies start to form. Over time these gullies can change the courses of various bodies of water.

On rare occasions, common hippos eat the duckweed that floats on the water's surface or dive underwater to reach plants that grow on the river floor. There have been reports of hippos eating other animals; some tell of hippos killing and feeding on a male impala. But these reports are rare and may be a result of hippos reacting to extreme conditions in their habitat, such as drought.

During their nightly grazing, common hippos eat anywhere from 88 to 150 pounds (40 to 68 kg) of plant matter. Although this sounds like a lot, it is only about 1% to 1.5% of their body weight. Many other hoofed animals eat about 2.5% of their body weight each day. Hippos don't need as much food because of their relaxed lifestyle. Hippos are most active at night during grazing time. They spend their days sleeping or moving slowly in the water, digesting food and getting rid of dung.

The hippo's stirred-up dung floats in the water. It is the basis for an entire food chain.

Common hippos stir up their dung while walking along the river bottom. The dung, because it has the thick consistency of wet hay, provides a good hiding place for insects. It is also food for snails and fish. These small organisms are then eaten by larger ones. Hippos are an important part of the African ecosystem. When they die in large numbers, the animals that depend on them die, too.

Pygmy hippos also feed at night along established paths marked by their dung. They eat water plants, fresh leaves from trees, fallen fruits, grasses, herbs, and ferns. Hippos eat these foods in a variety of ways. Pygmies graze grasses, strip leaves off branches, and pull swamp plants out of the ground. To reach high tree branches, they stand on their hind legs and brace themselves on the tree trunk using their forelegs. Pygmies spend their days hidden in swamps or sometimes in riverbank dens made by other animals that they enlarge for their own use.

A pygmy hippo grazes on grass.

Grooming

In some parts of Africa, fish and common hippos are close companions. The fish clean the hippos and eat the algae, parasites, and dead skin they scrape off. Different types of fish clean certain parts of the hippo. Labeo clean the hippo's hide and mouth using their large, rough tongues. Barbus feed on the hippo's dung and clean cracks in the soles of its feet. Cichlids clean the hippo's tail bristles, and Garra clean its wounds.

Hippos tend to gather in areas where there are many fish. It's as if they are offering themselves to be cleaned. They even move parts of their bodies to make it easier for the fish to get where they need to clean. Hippos keep their jaws open until the Labeo finish their cleaning. The Labeo need not fear the hippos' razor-sharp canine teeth. Hippos often become so relaxed during these cleanings that they fall asleep with their mouths open!

A Labeo fish cleans a common hippo's mouth.

Cattle egrets perch on a common hippo's back, looking for fish to catch.

Common hippos are tolerant of other animals, such as turtles and young crocodiles, which often lie on the hippos' backs and bask in the sun. Hammer-headed storks and cattle egrets use hippos as perches from which to fish. Ibises also perch on them, sometimes between their eyes. Hippos have been observed rolling over to expose the leeches attached to their bellies. When this happens, the ibis walks across the hippo's body and plucks the leeches off. Two or three ibises will take turns feeding on a hippo's leeches. The same hippos and ibises have been seen meeting at the same place and at the same time for days in a row. The ibises get fed, and the hippos get cleaned. What a deal!

19

At times, hippos take a more active role in their own grooming. As they wallow, or roll around in pools of mud, the water in the mud evaporates and cools their hides. The mud prevents flies from reaching their skin and also smothers parasites that are buried there. After the mud dries, hippos rub themselves against rough surfaces to remove dry skin and unwanted visitors.

Not much is known about the pygmy hippo's grooming habits, but it's thought that it, too, is visited by cleaning fish.

Social Organization and Behavior

Although some common hippos live alone, most live in herds, or bloats. There are groups with cows (female hippos) and calves (young hippos) called nursery herds, bachelor herds with all males, and mixed groups. The typical mixed group consists of 10 to 15 hippos. Usually one large bull (male hippo) leads a few cows, their calves, and a few young adult bulls. The large bull is thought to be the only one that mates with the cows in its herd.

Living together in herds provides protection. A young calf is less likely to be attacked by a crocodile if there are some adult hippos around. Hippos feel safer in the water than out, and a frightened hippo can be very dangerous. Away from the safety of the water, common hippos have been known to bite or trample anything that gets in their way. In any given year, hippos probably kill more people in Africa than any other wild animal.

This mixed group of common hippos includes a bull, cows, and calves.

Sometimes two bulls fight over the same territory. They threaten one another by opening their enormous mouths to display their huge canine teeth. The bulls scatter their dung with swishes of their tails. They lunge and dive, rear up and splash down, throw water using their mouths as buckets, or blow water through their nostrils. They also make sounds—usually a series of short, loud grunts and snorts. During some fights, these bulls make high-pitched squeals that can be heard for miles. Often, any one of these threats is enough to make the challenging hippo back off.

Sometimes, however, the threats don't work and the hippos fight. The fights can go on for hours and last until one of the bulls is seriously injured or dies from being slashed by the other's sharp lower tusks. Challenging a bull's territory is serious business. In an established environment, bulls can keep control of their territories for eight years or longer. But in less established environments, they might only stay in control for a few months.

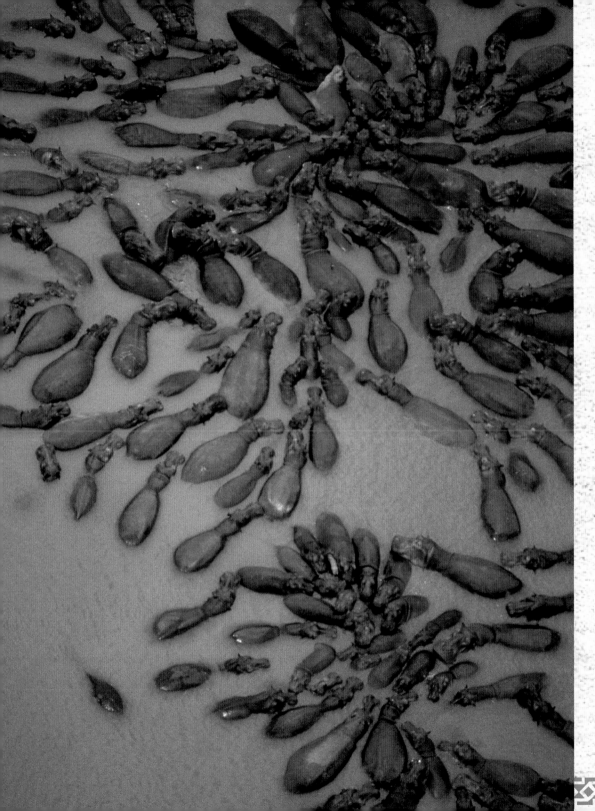

While bulls do fight over territory occasionally, most hippos stay in their own areas and avoid angering hippos in other herds. However, their behavior can change when food and water become scarce. During times of drought, large numbers of hippos (sometimes more than 100) from different herds are forced to gather near the sources of water that remain. These overcrowded conditions upset the balance of power between the herds and cause more aggression and fighting, especially among the oldest and strongest males.

A large number of hippos crowd together in the water. Drought conditions bring hippos from many bloats together. This often causes more fighting among the bulls.

Pygmy hippos live in smaller groups than do common hippos. They often live alone, or with one or two other hippos.

Pygmy hippos often live alone, in pairs, or in groups of three. Although their territories sometimes overlap, they don't appear to fight much among themselves. In fact, pygmy hippos seem to actually avoid one another. They can also become vicious when surprised by humans in their habitat. When they feel threatened, they usually hide in dense forests or sometimes in water.

Mating and Reproduction

Common hippos mate in the water during the dry season. Male hippos are ready to mate at age seven and females at age nine. The female carries her young for about seven and one-half months before it's born. She gives birth to one calf, on land or underwater, during the rainy season. Twins are rare. The calf, which weighs 75 to 100 pounds (34 to 45 kg), must rise quickly to the top of the water to take its first breath. It then closes its nostrils and resubmerges to nurse from its mother. A calf can only hold its breath underwater for about 30 seconds. While nursing it has to keep going up to the surface for air.

A hippo calf nurses underwater.

Mother hippos keep their calves close by.

The mother hippo is devoted to her calf. In the first days after birth, she takes her newborn into shallow water to protect it against all that come near, including crocodiles and even the male hippos in her herd! Male hippos don't bother the calves on land, but they've been known to attack them in the water and kill them. The hippo cow nurses her calf both on land and in the water.

The mother hippo keeps her calf close by on land, nudging it toward her if it strays.

When she and her calf rejoin the herd after a couple of weeks, the calf often climbs on the mother's back and suns itself while she rests in the water. This behavior may help to protect the young against crocodiles.

After rejoining the herd, the mother leaves her calf on the riverbank at night while she returns to the grazing paths with the rest of the herd. Because the calf is still nursing at this stage, it doesn't graze yet. Instead, it (along with other calves) is guarded by one or more cows. These cows act as babysitters, protecting the calves from hyenas, leopards, lions, and crocodiles.

At four to six months old, the calf begins to eat grass. Following close behind its mother, it finally joins the herd during the nightly grazing. The calf remains close to its mother for several years, even as she gives birth to more babies. It's not unusual to see a mother followed by four of her young.

These hippo calves will stay close by their mother for several years, even after she has given birth to more babies.

27

A mother pygmy hippo communicates with her calf.

Pygmy hippos start mating at age four or five. During the mating season, male pygmies seek out females, and they mate on land or in the water for a couple of days. The pygmy cow carries her baby for nearly seven months before giving birth to it on land. At birth, a pygmy calf weighs about eight pounds (3.6 kg). The calf is able to walk at birth but can only go short distances. The pygmy cow hides her calf in thick plant growth for long periods of time. She visits her concealed calf frequently to nurse it. Nursing takes place both on land and in the water.

Pygmy hippos can live in the wild up to 35 years and in captivity for 45 years.

Hippo Culture, Past and Present

Hippos have always been a part of the Nile River ecosystem. They played an important part in almost every aspect of ancient Egyptian life. Ancient Egyptian paintings show Pharaohs hunting hippos. The hippos' grazing paths helped to irrigate the land, their dung was used as a fertilizer, and their flesh provided Egyptians with oil and food.

Taweret was a popular ancient Egyptian symbol, pictured in both human and hippopotamus form. She represented motherhood and childbirth, and was a fierce fighter who guarded mothers and their newborns. The female hippo's protective maternal nature was an example of how to keep precious possessions safe. Taweret usually was shown with the body of a pregnant hippopotamus standing upright, the tail of a crocodile, and the paws of a lion. Sometimes she had a complete crocodile on her back, its jaws resting on top of her hippopotamus head. The hippo, crocodile, and lion are all extremely protective of their young.

Taweret's image has been found on ancient Egyptian women's cosmetic tools, headrests, and jewelry. Because of Taweret's protective powers, pregnant women often owned or carried charms with her image.

This ancient Egyptian wall painting shows Taweret, a pregnant hippo with the tail of a crocodile and the paws of a lion.

29

In addition to being worshipped by the ancient Egyptians, hippos have also had an impact on American culture. Hippos are often illustrated, photographed, and written about. In 1972, writer James Marshall started a popular series of children's books about a pair of hippos called George and Martha. Hippos are featured in cartoons, comic books, and movies, such as Walt Disney's *Fantasia*. Hippos are even used in advertising images and on greeting cards.

After learning something about these enormously interesting animals, it's difficult not to get caught up in "hippomania"—or to at least become inspired to learn more about them.

Glossary

adapted	to have changed in order to be able to live in a different situation
algae	types of scummy plants that are often red or brown, and that grow in water
drought	a long period of time when there isn't much rain
dung	an animal's solid waste
ecosystem	the relationships between all living and non-living things in a specific area
edible	safe to eat
fertilizer	a product that is added to the soil to help plants grow better
fossil	the hardened remains of a plant or animal that lived long ago
gullies	small valleys worn into the earth by running water
habitat	the area where an animal or plant naturally lives
impala	a type of antelope that lives in Africa
maternal	motherly
organism	any living thing
paleontologist	a type of scientist who learns about the past by studying fossils
parasite	a living thing that survives on or in another living thing
reserves	areas of land where the hunting of animals is not allowed
scarce	uncommon; not easy to get or find
species	a group of animals or plants that have many things in common
territory	the specific area in which an animal lives
wallow	to roll around in

Index